Echoes of Flight

Also by Jane Williams and published by Ginninderra Press
Begging the Question
Parts of the Main

Jane Williams

Echoes of Flight

haiku & senryu

Acknowledgements

Previously published in *brass bell: a haiku journal*, *DailyHaiga*, *tinywords*, *Chrysanthemum*, *cattails*, *Haiku News*, *Red Room Poetry*, *NeverEnding Story* (First English–Chinese bilingual haiku and tanka blog), *Failed Haiku (a Journal of English Senryu)*.

A number of these haiku have been translated into Hungarian, Slovak and Chinese.

Echoes of Flight: hailu & senryu
ISBN 978 1 76041 509 9
Copyright © Jane Williams 2018
Cover photo: Jane Williams

First published 2018 by
GINNINDERRA PRESS
PO Box 3461 Port Adelaide SA 5015
www.ginninderrapress.com.au

daytime moon – my first question – why

exchanging rare objects snail mail

cross-cultural her smile broadens with each mispronunciation

winter sun
bringing back to life
one side of my face

night bloomers
under the moon
we too open up

listening
to the ensemble
one lyrebird

red wine in the afternoon old photos come to life

neighbour's lawnmower turning up the volume *Star Trek*

riding a bike
after forty years
my childhood laugh

digital photo
you add light
until I appear

my father's country
each year he goes home
for the last time

morning swim once again water carries my weight

travelling without him passionfruit stains her white dress

low tide
in the gull's footprints
echoes of flight

filling
the rusted-out car
frog song

grounded boat
sea breeze stirring
its phantom sail

skinny dipping
my sister leads me
into my fiftieth year

bread baking the new house smells like home

first sip of coffee knocking over the cup

travelling
my dream world
becomes my world

twilight
birds shape-shifting
become one

at temple gate
selling warm lemonade –
Hanoi high season

floating village
the neighbours move
closer

sharing cake all the time in the world before the mammogram

café acoustics the pain in a stranger's voice

first light
making it look easy
to walk on water

landfill site the sun sinks lower

windy night I am tossed dream to dream

tourist trade
making a living
statues blink

peak hour shopping
lifting my feet
a stranger's laugh

early shift
taking in the sunrise
factory windows

dolphin pod so much more to see without my camera

outside the secondhand shop a single piece of jigsaw

imbedded
inside my daughter's text
another rainbow

company of ducks
when no one's looking
I quack back

haiku walk
we have to slow down
to catch up

winter solstice
counting my blessings
not enough hours today

at rest above the waterfall her walking cane

steaming pho the delicate aromas of a daydream

tower steps
climbing and counting
two different journeys

demolition site
the squatters move
in and out

oil-slicked ocean
too much time spent
washing hands

spring garden
her bare feet
grow shadows

homeless her shopping trolley overflows

beachcombing buoyed by each shell I leave

steam kettle
same old argument
boiling dry

a shiver
across water's skin
where platypus was

on the logging road
to fairy lake – how many
wishes make a tree?

a small smile the chemo nurse tries again

anniversary every german shepherd looks like yours

zen tea house –
each sip revealing
the next

alone in Paris
the temptation to
photoshop you in

writer's block
criss-crossing my keyboard
the same ant?

my breath caught by a dragonfly not landing

blank diary all the possible me's

still water reveals
the heron's twin –
head in the clouds

open window
the neighbour's music
inviting me

spring afternoon
the paper bark sheds
layers of light

googling my name still I can't find myself

dawn silhouette inside my falling dream my flying dream